ENDANGERED AND EXTINCT
ANIMALS OF THE
MOUNTAINS, DESERTS,
AND GRASSLANDS

Michael Bright

Copper Beech Books
Brookfield, Connecticut

© Aladdin Books Ltd 2002

Produced by:
Aladdin Books Ltd
28 Percy Street
London W1P 0LD

ISBN 0–7613–2712–6

First published in the United States in 2002 by:
Copper Beech Books,
an imprint of
The Millbrook Press
2 Old New Milford Road
Brookfield, Connecticut 06804

Editor:
Kathy Gemmell

Designers:
Flick, Book Design & Graphics
Simon Morse

Illustrators:
Peter Barrett, Tim Bramfitt,
Barry Croucher (Wildlife Art),
James Field (SGA),
Colin Howard (SGA),
Mick Loates, Stephen Sweet,
Mike Unwin, Ross Watton
(SGA), Maurice Wilson
Cartoons: Jo Moore

Certain illustrations have
appeared in earlier books
created by Aladdin Books.

Cataloging-in-Publication
data is on file at the
Library of Congress.

Contents

INTRODUCTION 3

ENDANGERED AND EXTINCT 4

LOST IN THE MOUNTAINS 6

BEAR NECESSITIES 8

MOUNTAIN BIRDS 11

MOUNTAIN CATS 12

DESERTED DESERTS 15

GIANTS OF THE PLAINS 16

VANISHING GRASSLAND BIRDS 19

RUN RABBIT RUN 21

LOSING THE BISON 22

GALLOPING TO EXTINCTION 24

WILD DOGS 27

DOWN TO EARTH 29

BACK FROM THE DEAD 30

GLOSSARY 31

INDEX 32

Introduction

Animals that live high in the mountains, in hot or cold deserts, or on the vast grasslands of the world often live in extreme conditions.

It can be very hot or very cold in these wild areas, with little shelter from the elements and few hiding places from predators. This means that there is a fine line between survival and death for many species. When the balance of life is upset by people arriving with guns or by destruction of habitats, the result can be catastrophic. Many species of animals living in mountains, deserts, and grasslands are now threatened with extinction.

 Q: Why watch for these boxes?

A: For answers to the animal questions you always wanted to ask.

 zoom in on... **Bits and pieces**

These boxes take a closer look at issues or the features of certain animals.

Awesome factS

Watch for these dodo diamonds to learn more about the weird and wonderful facts on endangered and extinct animals and their world.

Endangered and extinct

When few animals of a particular species survive in the wild, it is said to be endangered. If a species disappears altogether, it is extinct. Some extinctions are caused by human activities. Others are caused by natural events, like changes in climate or sea level, volcanic eruptions, or competition from similar animals.

SYMBOL DEFINITIONS
In this book, the red cross symbol shows an animal that is already extinct. The yellow exclamation shows an animal that is endangered. Animals that are less endangered are said to be "vulnerable." Those that are more endangered and close to extinction are considered to be "critically endangered." The green tick shows an animal that has either been saved from the brink of extinction or has recently been discovered. Many of these "success" stories, however, are still endangered species.

Blue buck

Takahe

California condor

Animals that have been introduced into a particular habitat, accidentally or on purpose, are called alien animals. Cats, for example, are taken overseas by humans to places where they do not occur naturally. If they breed, they attack and kill the resident animals and can cause them to become extinct.

Q: Does it matter if some animals become extinct?

A: Yes. Every plant and animal on Earth is important. Each has its role to play in the natural order. Removing one upsets the order and affects other living things. The overall picture of life on Earth—the variety of plants and animals, their behavior, and the ways in which they interact—is called biodiversity. Maintaining biodiversity is essential for the survival of all species.

The preservation of an animal's living space is critical for its survival. If its habitat is destroyed, it has nowhere to live and nothing to eat. Even if it is bred in captivity and released back into the wild, it will have difficulty surviving. This is what is happening to the giant panda. Its bamboo forests have been broken up and the species is now critically endangered.

For many years, people only hunted the wild animals they needed to survive. Then others started to kill too many animals, either for food or for fun. Bison, which once roamed the North American plains in huge herds, were shot by the million and some subspecies are now extinct.

Lost in the mountains

Many wild animals once found refuge high in the mountains. In these remote places, they were safely isolated from people. But, as in all the world's wilderness areas, humans moved into the mountains, and they brought their guns with them. Now, animals in even the remotest mountainous regions are no longer safe.

The walia ibex is a mountain goat that lives on steep cliffs in the Simien Mountains of Ethiopia. It is hunted for its meat and hide, and its horns are treasured locally as drinking vessels.

!

The markhor lives along the tree line in the mountains of India and Pakistan, where it competes for food and territory with domestic goats. It is also hunted for its horns, which are used as ingredients in oriental medicine. The horns can be sold for nearly $500 per pound.

Markhor

There are 12 million domestic yaks in the Himalayas, but only a few hundred wild yaks. They are confined to the Tibetan plateau and nearby areas. Attempts are being made to conserve the surviving wild yak in order to revitalize the domestic stock.

Bear necessities

Bears are strong, hardy carnivores that have adapted to eating plant material. Their fur is thick and luxurious, and this has been their downfall. Hunters have killed bears for their pelt (furry skin), and many are now endangered or extinct.

Awesome facts

Between 1974 and 1976, the bamboo in the Min Mountains of China flowered and died back. At least 138 giant pandas starved to death.

Red panda

The red panda is not actually a bear. It is related to raccoons, but lives in the mountain forests of western and southwestern China, just like the giant panda, which is a bear. Both species are endangered through loss of habitat.

Atlas bear

zoom in on...

Captive breeding programs

Pandas have been doing so badly in the wild that the Chinese authorities are trying to breed them in captivity, and then return them to the wild. Unfortunately, the bamboo that they eat remains only in isolated fragments of the forest, and farms separate these. This means that if all the bamboo in one part of the forest flowers and withers, there are no nearby bamboo forests for the pandas to move to, so they starve.

The Atlas bear was the only bear to live in Africa, in the Atlas Mountains. Its mountain forests were gradually cut down, and it was brought to fight in the arenas of ancient Rome. It survived until about 1870, when widespread use of guns sealed its fate. It is now extinct.

Lear's macaw

!

Lear's macaw is a critically endangered species, due to an illegal pet trade. The 200 survivors live in the desert plateaus and canyons of Bahia, Brazil, where they eat the nuts of the licuri palm.

In the tussock grasses of New Zealand's mountains, lives the takahe, a flightless bird of the rail family. They were thought to be extinct in 1930, killed by European stoats, but were rediscovered in 1948. About 150 survive today.

!

Takahe

zoom in on...

Too few

The critically endangered Hawaiian crow is close to extinction. There are no more than 12 in the wild and 10 in captivity. Rats killed the rest. Recovery is unlikely because there are too few birds and inbreeding would make the birds weak and vulnerable to disease.

but they will also eat the occasional insect.

The Himalayan mountain quail is extinct. It once lived in the foothills of the Himalayas, and was so well camouflaged that a hiker could almost step on it before it fled. The last one was seen in 1868.

Mountain birds

Birds on mountains and moors are usually well camouflaged to avoid being seen by predators. Some change their plumage to blend in with snow in winter and the plants in summer. If their habitat is destroyed, the birds have nowhere to hide and are easily killed.

Mountain cats

Cats are impressive killers, but many are themselves hunted. Some are killed to make coats from their beautiful fur, others because they eat domestic livestock. Some of the biggest are shot purely for sport.

Just 1,200 Iberian lynx survive in Spain. These small cats eat rabbits, but numbers fell when there was disease in the rabbit population. Today, land clearance and building projects have badly affected lynx numbers.

!

Q: Why was lion-hunting so popular?

A: Lions are big, powerful cats, and males look spectacular with their huge mane. Many lions were captured to fight gladiators in ancient Rome in arenas packed with spectators.

!

The endangered snow leopard in the mountains of central Asia is hunted for its luxurious fur. Its bones are also used in oriental medicine. It eats wild sheep and goats, but they are also becoming rare.

in fur to help it run over snow.

The Barbary lion lived in the forested areas of North Africa. It was the largest and most impressive subspecies of lion, and was heavily hunted. The male measured up to 10 feet (3 m) from its nose to the tip of its tail, and had a mane that covered almost half of its body. It survived until 1922, when the last true Barbary lion was killed.

Barbary lion

Scimitar-horned oryx live in waterless areas in the subdeserts between the Sahara and the Sahel in Africa. Few survive today, because climate change and overhunting have brought the species to the edge of extinction. One herd has been introduced to southern Tunisia and numbers there are beginning to recover.

Scimitar-horned oryx

14

Only 250 wild bactrian camels survive in central Asia's Gobi Desert. They are the only truly wild, two-humped camels in the world. Thick eyelashes, nostrils that close, and broad feet enable them to live in sandy desert.

zoom in on...

Oryx revival

The Arabian oryx is a reintroduction success story. A few were captured in 1962 and raised in captivity. The last wild oryx died in 1972, but since 1980, oryx have been released in Oman and into reserves in the Middle East.

Deserted deserts

Deserts have always been tough places to live in. But when local hunters got four-wheel drive vehicles and automatic weapons, many desert animals were quickly wiped out. Some species survived in captivity and have been bred and rereleased.

Giants of the plains

The grasslands are a dangerous place to be, but less so if you are big. The largest land mammals in Africa include the elephant and rhinoceros, but even they are helpless when faced with poachers' guns.

There are several types of African elephant. Some live in the bush, while others live in the desert or forest. Wherever they live, their habitat is shrinking rapidly. Confinement to isolated game parks has disrupted their long-distance migrations.

Elephants are killed for their huge ivory tusks. These are shipped to the Far East, where they are turned into carved jewelry and ornaments. The demand for ivory is so high that illegal hunting is likely to wipe out some elephant populations.

Only 2,500 black rhinos survive in isolated pockets of African bush. The black rhino is a browser (eats leaves), while its relative, the white rhino, is a grazer (eats grass). Both are killed for their horns.

Q: Why are rhinos killed for their horns?

A: Rhino horn is used in oriental medicine and is very highly valued. It is also used to make traditional dagger handles in Yemen. It is so valuable that rhino horn is worth more than its weight in gold. In many reserves, poaching patrols have been set up to stop the illegal killing of rhinos for their horns.

Heath hens once lived on open, dry land in New England, but they were shot by the thousand by settlers from Europe. Fatal diseases introduced by domestic chickens and pheasants killed many more. The species was extinct on the mainland by 1830, but a few survived on the protected island of Martha's Vineyard. The last one died in 1932.

Vanishing grassland birds

Grassland and heath birds are particularly vulnerable to bush fires, weather, and natural predators, but they can also be easy targets for hunters. Some species that were once common were hunted to extinction in a very short time.

The Florida grasslands were once home to painted vultures. They were scavengers. Severe winter frosts in the 1700s weakened the population, but settlement by humans finally caused their extinction.

Awesome facts

Large numbers of painted vultures used to soar over grass fires. The birds swooped in to feed on animals that were roasted in the flames.

19

The short-tailed chinchilla lives high in South America's Andes Mountains. Its luxurious fur is highly valued and the animals have been overhunted. The wild population declined by more than 80 percent in the 1990s.

Mexican prairie dog

Domestic cattle and horses can break their legs in the burrows of small mammals, so ranch owners try to get rid of them, usually by poisoning. In this way, the Mexican prairie dog has been poisoned almost into extinction.

The Sumatran rabbit is the world's rarest rabbit. It lives in remote mountain forests, where tea and coffee plantations are replacing natural forests. There has been only one sighting since 1916.

Run rabbit run

Rabbits and other small mammals have been reared in captivity for their meat and fur since ancient times. Their wild relatives, however, are sometimes considered pests and meet an early death through poisoning or trapping.

Biological control

Releasing wild predators to control pests—called biological control—can sometimes go wrong. In New Zealand, ferrets and stoats were used to kill introduced rabbits, but they also killed many other animals, including rare flightless birds and their chicks.

zoom in on...

21

Losing the bison

In North America in the 1800s, bison herds were so big that it took settlers three days to ride through a herd. But as soon as they were found, they were slaughtered for trophies, meat, and hides. Between 1850 and 1880, 75 million hides were sold.

Q: Who saved the bison?

A: In the late 1800s, bison were massacred, some shot from specially chartered trains. By 1900, just 541 animals were left. Then, in 1905, the American Bison Society was formed. Its members saved two of the four U.S. subspecies. Most bison alive today are Great Plains bison.

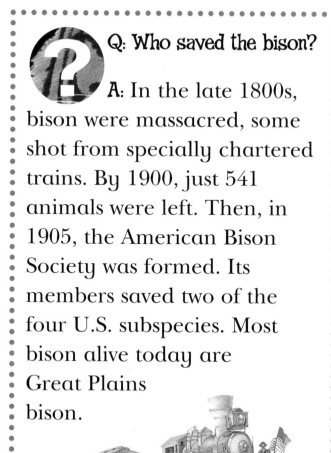

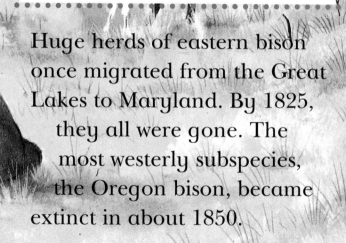

Huge herds of eastern bison once migrated from the Great Lakes to Maryland. By 1825, they all were gone. The most westerly subspecies, the Oregon bison, became extinct in about 1850.

Europe has its own species of bison, the mountain and lowland wisents. The shy lowland wisent still survives in reserves in Poland, but the mountain wisent (right) is extinct due to hunting and forest destruction.

Eastern bison

Awesome factS

"Buffalo Bill" Cody claimed to have shot the most bison, or buffalo, of anyone. He killed 4,862 in one year, which is an average of 13 a day!

Galloping to extinction

Horses and antelope rely on speed to escape from their predators, but they cannot flee a bullet. Horses were domesticated over 5,000 years ago by people, so although the truly wild horse is extinct, many of its genes are preserved, hidden away in domestic breeds.

Grevy's zebra is the most primitive species of living zebra and is recognized by its narrow stripes. It lives in the semi-arid scrub of Ethiopia and northern Kenya, and is threatened by competition from domestic animals. It is also hunted for its skin and meat.

!

Grevy's zebra

New old breeds

The tarpan was a wild horse of the forests and grasslands in eastern Europe and western Asia. It is extinct, but attempts are being made to breed it back from its domestic descendants, such as the primitive Konik horses of Poland, Iceland ponies, and Gotland ponies from Sweden. These new herds of "tarpan" have been reintroduced to the Bialowieza Forest in Poland.

The last wild Przewalski's horse of central Asia was seen in 1968. Several have been kept and bred in zoos, and some are being returned to the wild in reserves in Mongolia.

Blue buck

The South African blue buck was easy to stalk and shoot, and was the first African animal to become extinct since prehistoric times. Its hide was the color and texture of fine blue velvet.

The Tasmanian wolf, or thylacine, was a marsupial predator. Like the wolf, it was thought to kill sheep and was shot. The last wild one was caught in 1933. Since then, there have been no confirmed sightings.

Wild dogs

Dogs and wolves are pack hunters, and are able to bring down prey much larger than themselves. Despite being "man's best friend," many species, such as coyotes, foxes, and wolves, are considered pests and are poisoned or shot.

Newfoundland white wolves were a large species that measured up to 6 $\frac{1}{2}$ feet (2 m) in length. In 1911, it was the first North American wolf to become extinct.

Many African wild dogs have been killed because they are considered a threat to livestock. They are also vulnerable to diseases carried by domestic dogs, and have disappeared from 25 of the 39 countries they once lived in.

Newfoundland white wolf

Q: Why is Round Island so special?

A: Round Island is a tiny island in the Indian Ocean with more endangered plants and animals per acre than anywhere else on Earth. Conservation measures have been introduced to save the survivors. Lizards and snakes have been bred in captivity then released into the wild.

Madagascar

Round island

Mauritius

Madagascar

There is only one Round Island boa left. It cannot breed, so the species is effectively extinct. Rabbits and goats introduced in 1844 destroyed the plant cover in which it hides. Storms washed away the topsoil in which it burrows, leaving gullies 30 feet (9 m) deep in places.

Awesome facts

A predatory snail introduced to South Pacific islands to control escaped African land snails ate the local Partula snails instead, which are now threatened with extinction.

The Corsican snail was rediscovered in 1995, having not been seen since 1902. Only 17 acres of suitable snail habitat survives and even this is threatened by airport and resort development.

Down to earth

Extinction is not confined to the big animals. Many small creatures are in trouble, too. Snails, ants, beetles, butterflies, and dragonflies all appear on lists of endangered or extinct animals.

The most ancient species of living ant is the dinosaur ant of South Australia. It was alive when dinosaurs ruled the Earth. In 1977, colonies of these ants were discovered living in a small area of land on the Eyre Peninsula.

Back from the dead

Animals on the brink of extinction are being saved, but sometimes the conservation techniques used are unusual. Freezing the fertilized eggs of a rare species and implanting them later in mothers of related, more common species is one way to relieve the stress of birth in the endangered species.

 Q: Who decides when an animal is endangered?

A: The IUCN (International Union for the Conservation of Nature and Natural Resources) coordinates research about surviving plant and animal families. The status of each species is assessed and the findings are published in Red Data Books. The buying, selling, hunting, and poaching of wild animals is monitored by CITES (Convention on International Trade in Endangered Species of Wild Fauna and Flora).

A successful captive breeding program to save the California condor uses birdlike glove puppets to feed the young birds. This means that when the birds are released, they do not associate humans with food. California condors are now being released into the Grand Canyon wilderness area of Arizona.

Glossary

biological control
The use of a plant, animal, or microscopic living form to control the numbers of another animal or plant that has become a pest.

camouflage
The way in which an animal hides from predators by blending with its surroundings.

captive breeding
The breeding of animals in zoos and parks to preserve endangered species.

carnivore
An animal that eats meat.

domestic animals
Animals that have been bred and looked after by people.

endangered
Describes a species which is likely to die out if the factors causing its decline continue.

extinct
Describes a species that has not been seen in the wild for 50 years or more.

habitat
The place where an animal lives, usually characterized by the plants that grow there.

inbreeding
Breeding with closely related individuals, which often results in weak breeding stock and diseased young.

introduced
Describes a species brought by humans into a habitat where it does not occur naturally.

mammal
A backboned animal with hair, such as a cat or a human, which feeds its young on milk.

migration
The movement of animals to and from their winter feeding grounds and their summer breeding and feeding grounds.

oriental medicine
A form of medicine from the

Far East that uses parts of plants and animals to help prevent or cure diseases.

plantation
An area of trees or other plants that people plant in order to harvest their wood, leaves, or fruits.

population
A group of individuals of the same type.

predator
An animal that hunts and eats other animals.

scavenger
A meat eater that eats dead animals, often killed by others.

species
A group of animals that resemble each other and are able to breed together.

subspecies
Animals of the same species that have developed their own characteristics, often because they have been separated from others with which they could breed.

31

Index

alien animals 4
American Bison Society 22
antelope 24
ants, dinosaur 29

bamboo 5, 8, 9
bears 8
  Atlas 8, 9
beetles 29
biodiversity 4, 5
biological control 21, 31
birds 10, 11, 19, 21, 30, 31
bison 5, 22, 23
  eastern 22, 23
  Great Plains 22
  Oregon 22
blue buck 4, 25
boas, Round Island 28
bones 12
breeding 4, 25, 28, 31
  captive 5, 9, 15, 21, 28,
    30, 31
browsers 17
buffalo 23
butterflies 29

camels, bactrian 15
camouflage 11, 31
carnivores 8, 31
cats 4, 12, 31
cattle 20
chickens 18
chinchillas, short-tailed 20
CITES 30
climate 4, 14
Cody, "Buffalo Bill" 23
competition 4, 7, 24
condor, California 4, 30
conservation 7, 28, 30
coyotes 27
crows, Hawaiian 10

dinosaurs 29
diseases 10, 12, 18, 27, 31
dogs 27
  African wild 26, 27
  Mexican prairie 20
domestic animals 7, 12, 18,
  20, 24, 25, 27, 31
dragonflies 29

elephants 16
  African 16

ferrets 21
fires 19
foxes 27
fur 8, 12, 13, 20, 21

goats 6, 7, 12, 28
grazers 17

habitats 3, 4, 5, 8, 11, 16,
  29, 31
hens, heath 18
hermaphrodites 28
hides 6, 22, 25
horns 6, 7, 16, 17
horses 20, 24, 25
  Konik 25
  Przewalski's 25
hunting 5, 6, 7, 8, 12, 13,
  14, 15, 16, 19, 20, 23, 24,
  26, 30

ibex, walia 6
inbreeding 10, 31
insects 11
introduced (animals) 4, 14,
  21, 28, 29, 31
IUCN 30
ivory tusks 16

leopards, snow 12
lions 12, 13
  Barbary 13
lizards 28
lynx, Iberian 12

macaws, Lears 10
mammals 16, 20, 21, 31
markhors 7
migration 16, 22, 31

oriental medicine 7, 12, 17,
  31
oryx 15
  Arabian 15
  scimitar-horned 14

pandas 9
  giant 5, 8, 9
  red 8
pelts 8
pet trade 10
pheasants 18
plantations 21, 31
poaching 16, 17, 30
poisoning 20, 21, 27
ponies
  Gotland 25
  Iceland 25
populations 12, 16, 19, 20, 31
predators 3, 11, 19, 21, 24,
  26, 29, 31
prey 27

quails, Himalayan
  mountain 11

rabbits 12, 21, 28
  Sumatran 21
raccoons 8

rails 10
rats 10
Red Data Books 30
reintroduction 15, 25
reserves 15, 23, 25
rhinoceroses 16, 17
  black 17
  white 17

scavengers 19, 31
sea level 4
sheep 12, 26
snails 28, 29
  African land 29
  Corsican 29
  Partula 29
snakes 28
species 3, 4, 5, 8, 14, 15, 18,
  19, 23, 24, 27, 28, 30, 31
stoats 21
  European 10
subspecies 5, 13, 22, 31

takahes 4, 10
tarpans 25
thylacines 26

vultures, painted 19

wisents
  lowland 23
  mountain 23
wolves 26, 27
  Newfoundland white 27
  Tasmanian 26

yaks 6, 7

zebras 24
  Grevy's 24
zoos 25, 31